Salt Pond Sleuths

Heron Brothers Encourage Conservation

by Ardith M. Schneider

A portion of the proceeds from this book will be donated to the Salt Ponds Coalition of Rhode Island.

FACT: The southern shore of Rhode Island is home to nine major salt ponds.

Here we are brothers two;
this is Harry and I am Hugh.
I am older. My feathers are more blue;
Harry's are duller, a brownish hue.
We have a mission fighting pollution.
We explore the salt ponds
to find a solution.

Hugh is a big shot.
He talks a lot.
I'm just learning,
so I do not.

FACT: Young herons are brownish gray with a black cap. As they get older, they are bluish gray.

Many herons like to roam,
but we claim the salt ponds as our home.
We love to wade in this scenic place
and see what's been done by the human race.
Sometimes it's good.   Sometimes it's bad.
So when we see clear water like this -
we're really glad!

FACT: Herons are called partial migrators because some migrate and others do not.

One way we herons see a lot
is by standing still in just one spot.
What helped me see even more
were the glasses I found in litter on shore.
When I put them on, I was so astounded -
my vision clear, and so compounded!

Good for you, Hugh.

FACT: Herons can see very well at night because of many photoreceptors in their eyes.

Now, with my 20/20 sight,
I look for things that just aren't right.
Trash on the shore or a source of pollution -
we want nothing more
than to find a solution.

Awk! Awk!

Fact: Heron sounds are like a loud hoarse squawk, awk, fraunk or croak.

Why does the water look yucky like that? There's stuff in here like a floating mat.

That's algae - a plant that runs amok. It fouls the water and smells like YUCK! It depletes the O_2 in H_2O and adds to the environment's woe. Low oxygen can kill fish, crabs and bass and underwater plants called eelgrass.

FACT: H_2O is the chemical formula for water, and O_2 is the oxygen that is dissolved in it and so important to marine animals.

Well,
when eelgrass dies off, it's quite bad, I must say.
No place for our friends to lay eggs, hide or play -
just algal mats lying there to decay.

Hugh, continue with your lecture.
You have learned so much as our
inspector.

FACT: Algae will grow until it runs out of nitrate. If there are very high levels of nitrate in the water, algae can grow unchecked. This is called an algal bloom which makes the water murky and also makes it hard for eelgrass to grow.

NITRATE, Harry, that's the offender.
It can rob a pond of health and splendor.
It comes to a salt pond in liquid form -
in groundwater or runoff during a storm.

Just how did this happen to our ponds so dear?
All we want is to see our water crystal clear!

FACT: When algae dies it sinks, decomposes (breaks down), and becomes part of the pond bottom.
Decomposition uses up oxygen in the water, so after an algal bloom, oxygen levels get very low.
Without enough oxygen crabs, shellfish and fish struggle to survive.

Now that we know a few of the basics, let's fly off to see some really cool places. We'll start at the western end of the state and see how the ponds are doing to date.

Let's get going; I can't wait. You lead the way, Hugh, and I will navigate!

FACT: Maschaug, Card's and Trustom Ponds are brackish - they are more salty than freshwater but less salty than the ocean. How salty they are depends on how recently they were connected to the ocean by a break in the barrier beach.

Hugh,
'glad you're flying at a slower rate.
I can see all the ponds and lakes in
this *Ocean State*.

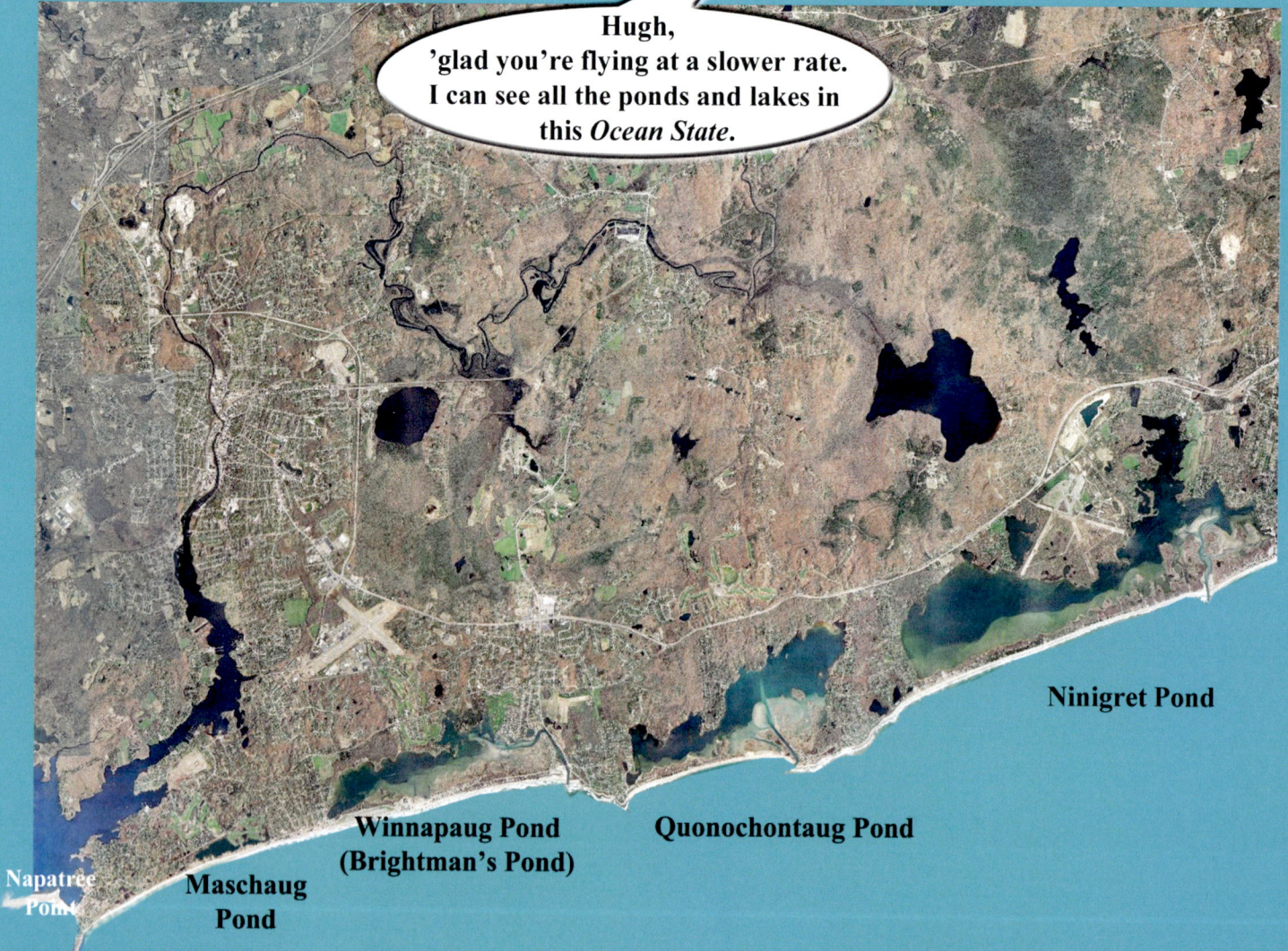

Ninigret Pond

Winnapaug Pond
(Brightman's Pond)

Quonochontaug Pond

Napatree
Pond

Maschaug
Pond

FACT: Great blue herons can cruise at 20 to 30 miles per hour.

We'll fly up high to get an overview.
West to east is the thing to do.
Then we'll swoop down low as we turn back -
landing at Maschaug, right on track.

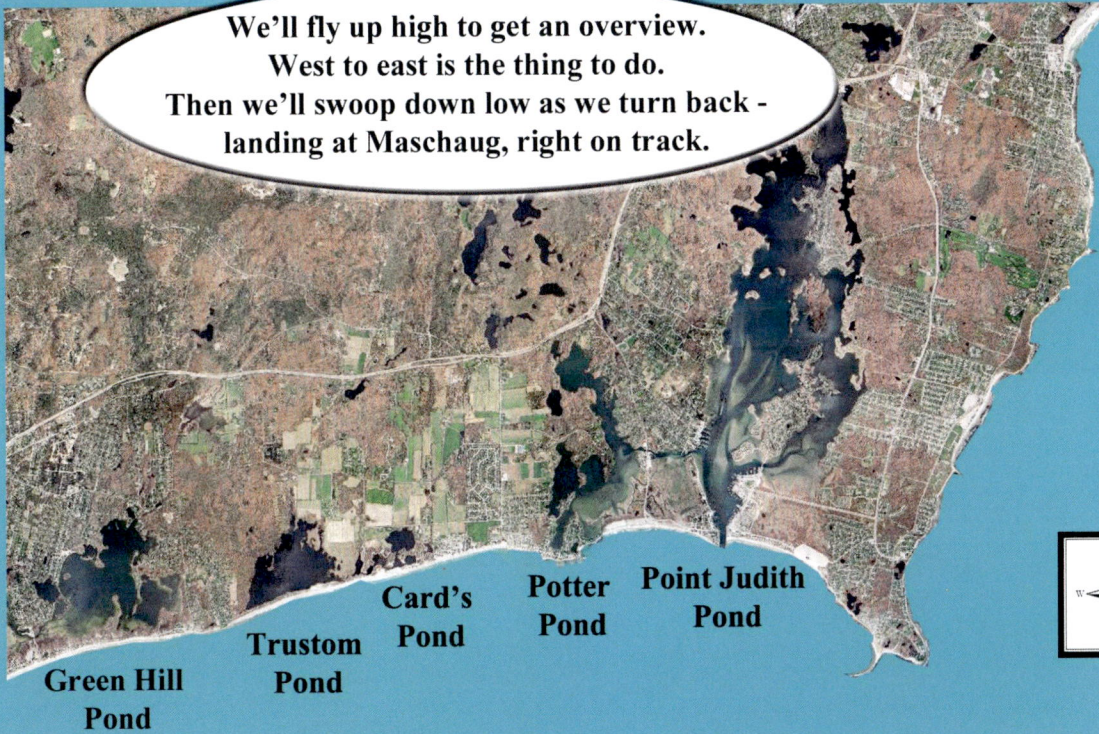

Green Hill Pond

Trustom Pond

Card's Pond

Potter Pond

Point Judith Pond

FACT: Rhode Island's greatest width from east to west is 37 miles, but it has more than 400 miles of shoreline.

RIGIS, URI EDC, RIDEM

RIGIS

Watch Hill's the first place on our list.
Maschaug Pond is so small it's easily missed.
You see it's bordered by a long stretch of beach.
Let's fly over there - it's not out of reach.
The piping plover has nests protected here.
We wouldn't want these little birds to disappear.

Here East Beach faces Block Island Sound.
Some of the waves crashing really astound!

FACT: Southeast of East Beach is a mile-long conservation peninsula, Napatree Point. It provides a year-round habitat for many wildlife species and a stopover site for migratory birds.

FACT: Eelgrass is a very important part of a healthy salt pond habitat and needs clean, clear water to grow.

FACT: The enhancement of wildlife habitats and advice on sustainable resource management are two of the benefits of becoming an Audubon Cooperative Sanctuary.

Now look over here at this special device.
The job it does is really quite nice.
It treats wastewater that goes down the drain
and makes it much more like falling rain.
And that nitrogen pollution, of which we are wary,
helps clean it up, my brother Harry!

And, Hugh, the septic systems are pretty cool.
They use good bacteria as their tool.

FACT: Traditional functioning septic systems treat bacteria, but do little to reduce nitrogen entering the groundwater. Denitrifying systems help reduce nitrogen levels in well water, wetlands and the salt ponds.

Flying from Winnipaug, now in wading mode,
we go east to this cove by Weekapaug Road.
See the geese as we follow our route;
in large numbers, they too pollute.
They eat on a golf course or a lawn or beyond
and do their business back at the pond.

All the nutrients the geese transport
bring in more nitrogen than the
ponds can support.

FACT: Landowners can discourage large flocks of geese by planting native shrubs and
grass buffers along the edges of the ponds.

16

Quonnie Pond is next, and its waters are rich.
There's eelgrass here as well as tasty fish!
On the bottom are scallops, oysters and clams -
treats that many have in their plans.

Maybe if we sit in a straddle,
our wings will be long enough to paddle.
And we could go out where it's deep
and fly off with a great big leap!

FACT: "Quonnie" is the nickname for Quonochontaug which means "place of the black fish".

Here we are at the breach, whoopee!
The tide flushes water out from the pond to the sea.
Of course the opposite happens too
when salt water from the ocean rushes through.
A lot depends on the wind and the waves.
It's hard to predict just how the sea behaves.

Look behind you, Hugh,
there's a young bald eagle.
He's handsome and rare
and oh, so regal.

FACT: The breachways in Winnapaug, Quonochontaug, Ninigret and Point Judith Ponds are manmade and allow for boats to pass and water to flush in and out.

Hold on a sec, Harry, don't hurry.
I'm using my glasses so it's not blurry.
Aha, I've spotted something olive drab.
It's the ancient horseshoe crab.
These living fossils are incredibly old,
450 million years, or so I am told.

There are oysters here,
too, numbering three.
Let's go to where they are
being farmed, agree?

FACT: Horseshoe crabs, which can live between 30 and 40 years, breed in the salt ponds and come and go through the breachways. They are largely unchanged from prehistoric times, predating T-Rex by 150 million years.

FACT: One adult oyster can filter up to 30 gallons of water per day!

Ninigret Pond is the largest, you see.
There's so much life and diversity.
In May on the shores of Ninigret Park
there are cinder worms hatching just after dark.
It's a well-known event that brings many striped bass.
They find them so tasty, they just can't pass.

But Hugh, there are lots of other things that people do,
like kayaking, fishing and clamming, too.

FACT: Cinder worms, also called clam worms, are red and about 5 inches long. They are quite a spectacle as they twist and dart in the water.

Flying in to Green Hill, such a pretty place -
separated from Ninigret by just a small space.
It can't get clean water directly from the sea,
which causes Green Hill problems aplenty.

There can be a high bacteria count -
a problem that's been hard to surmount.
However it's a great place for kayaking and birding, too.
That means some people are probably
looking up at you!

FACT: Shellfishing is not allowed in Green Hill Pond (since 1994) due to bacterial contamination. The pond is deemed safe for recreational activities.

FACT: Great blue herons nest in colonies, called "rookeries." Herons build their nests in trees close to feeding areas. They can be seen around the ponds more often in mid-summer after their chicks are able to fly.

Trustom Pond is a place we hang out a lot.
It's a wildlife refuge, a pretty quiet spot.
There are marshes and meadows and trails to trek,
and even this neat observation deck.

Hugh,
I'm looking around from west to east.
With this telescope my vision has increased.
I see lots of our feathered friends -
really up close with this zoom lens.

FACT: Managed by the U. S. Fish and Wildlife Service, this is the only undeveloped pond in the state.

Card's Pond is clean; there's no debris.
There's so little beach between it and the sea.
It's a pond that's breached intentionally
because flooding occurs so frequently.

The pond is larger than we're perceiving.
Little fingers of land go into it which is deceiving.

FACT: Several times a year Card's Pond is breached to prevent flooding, sometimes with the help of the U. S. Fish and Wildlife Service.

As we wade and fly over this north end of Potter, we can't see the bottom through the deep, dark water. But once we get to the south end, the water's more clear and the last pond, Point Judith, is very near!

Well, Hugh, it seems to me there's something different about Potter Pond. Agree? I've noticed its shape with the shore goes vertically. And when I look at the map, I can see that perfectly.

FACT: A tidal inlet connects the middle of Potter Pond to Point Judith Pond - the only way Potter Pond exchanges water with the ocean (see map, page 11).

Hugh, what is being collected over there? The human seems to be taking precise care.

He's a "citizen scientist" - doing some inspecting. Every two weeks, he's out there collecting. With the results they are able to tell more about the health of the water and trends as well.

FACT: About 30 pondwatchers with the Salt Ponds Coalition collect water samples from the salt ponds and compile the results in a format that is easy for researchers to use.

Now that we've flown back and forth, we have reached Point Judith, looking north. They must be farming oysters in this pond, too. Shells were left here. See them, Hugh?

I see them, Harry. There are several oyster farms near here. Their feeding helps make the water clear. Remember how I told you they pump water through their innards? And they filter out algae - that makes their dinners.

FACT: Oyster farming has many benefits: improved habitat for fish and birds, water filtration and improved water quality, and jobs for oyster farmers.

28

Well, Harry,
I might have told you more than is necessary.
There are so many places along this Point Judith estuary.
A river runs in from way up and beyond
and carries contaminants down into the pond.
There are marinas and ferries, a big fishing port -
creating too many pollutants for this pond
to support.

So like all the ponds about which we care
there needs to be a big effort
while there's something to repair.
AND
wouldn't it be nice if we all did our share?

FACT: Point Judith Pond is an estuary - an inlet of the sea at the lower end of a river.

So, Harry, from beach to marsh and pond to bay, which do you like best, of these ponds we surveyed?

It's hard to say, each is special in its own way. Rather than choosing, how about we just fly away to the pond that catches our fancy each day?

FACT: The salt ponds of Rhode Island are a regional treasure. They support productive habitats and diverse wildlife as well as public recreation and enhanced property values.

Glossary

Bacteria - microscopic single-celled organisms.

Barrier beach - a strip of land that separates salt pond from ocean, with the beach on the ocean side, dunes in the middle and salt marsh or beach along the pond side.

Breach - a natural or mechanically made channel going through a barrier from ocean to pond.

Buffer zone (conservation) - a border of vegetated land designed to protect wetlands and bodies of water from storm water runoff.

Contaminant - a substance that pollutes or spoils something.

Decomposition - a natural process of breaking down organic matter into its base components.

Denitrifying - the loss or removal of nitrates - chemical compounds that contain nitrogen and oxygen and are found in fertilizer and wastewater.

Deplete - to lose most or all of something, like eelgrass.

Eutrophication - the process in which a body of water becomes enriched with nutrients that stimulate the growth of algae and phytoplankton, resulting in the depletion of dissolved oxygen and a decline in aquatic health.

Lagoon - an enclosed area of seawater that has a modest connection to the ocean and minimal fresh water input.

Migrate - the action of birds and other wildlife as they go from one region or place to another, usually based on time of year and lifecycle.

Osprey - a large fish-eating hawk, found throughout the world.

Photoreceptors - a group of cells specialized to receive light.

Birds seen in photo:
Snowy egrets in background, American oystercatchers (red-orange bill) and dunlins in the foreground.

31

Can you answer these questions?

1. Do great blue herons see well at night?
2. What underwater plant creates a very important habitat in the salt ponds?
3. Which salt pond is actually an estuary?
4. What nutrient is responsible for making algae grow in the salt ponds?
5. Which salt pond is managed by the U. S. Fish and Wildlife Service?
6. What do oysters filter out of the water?
7. What salt pond is home to a large fishing port?
8. Which salt pond is the largest?
9. Which salt pond is the smallest?
10. What are advanced septic systems better at removing than the old ones?

Something to think about: What can kids do to help the salt ponds? What can a community do to help the salt ponds? **(See back cover)**

Acknowledgments

OVER AND ABOVE - Elise Torello, Executive Director, Salt Ponds Coalition; and Mark Bullinger, Naturalist, Weekapaug Inn.
Thank you for your expertise, photographs and rhymes.
EDITING - Helen Jankoski, Jim Morris and Liz Sayre
Thank you for your help with grammar, ideas and style.

Salt Ponds Coalition Committee: Mark Bullinger, Art Ganz, Bill Lester, Kristin and Anna Revill and Elise Torello.

The Tidal Page, newletters of the Salt Ponds Coaltion, and the website www.saltpondscoalition.org were the main sources of information for this book.

www.ArdiSchneider.com   Available on Amazon.com

Made in the USA
Lexington, KY
20 August 2017